JEM

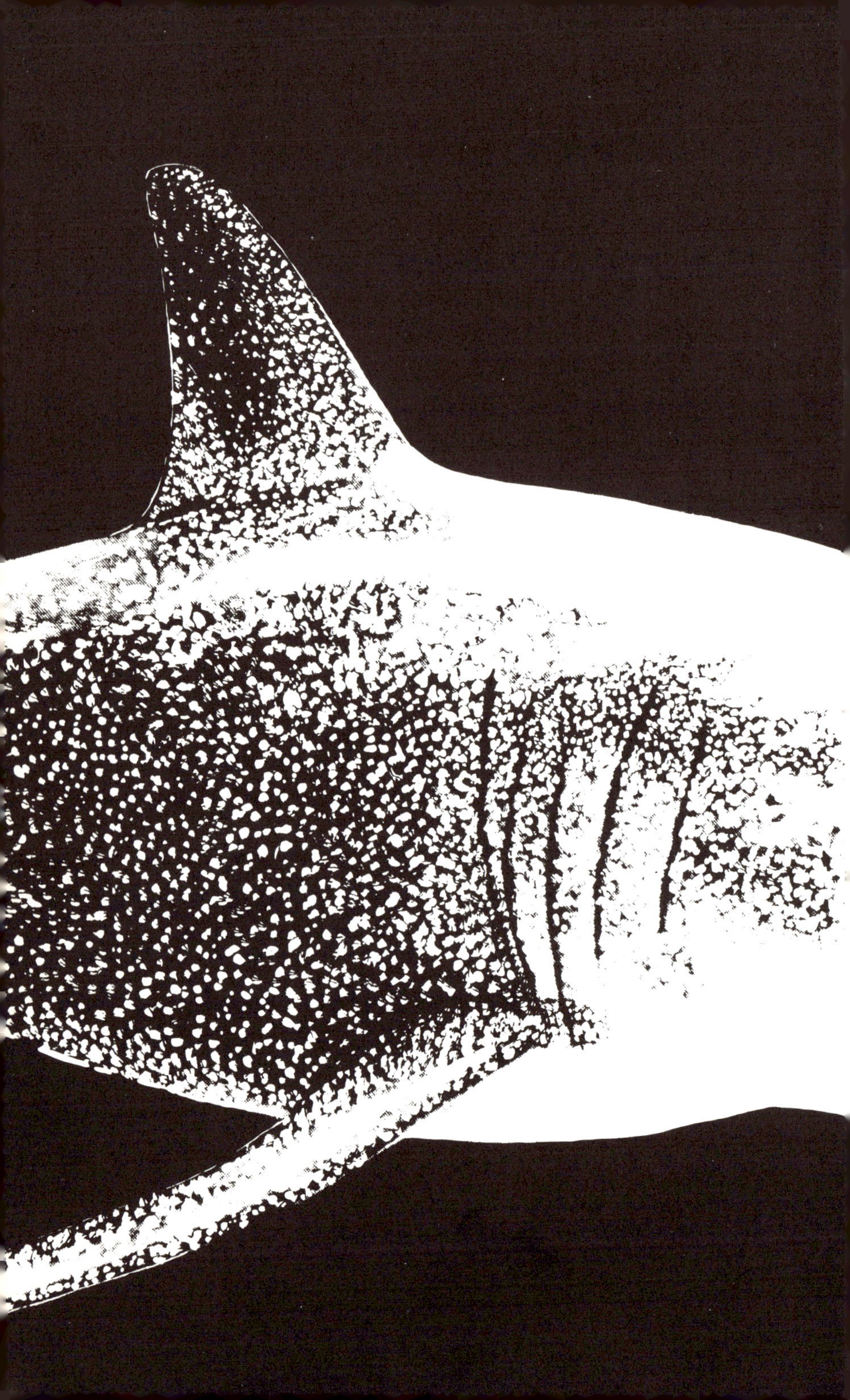

# THE GREAT WHITE SHARK

EVE BUNTING

JULIAN MESSNER • NEW YORK

A JEM BOOK

Picture Credits: Courtesy American Museum of Natural History, pages 8, 11, 12, 17 (bottom), 18-20, 50, 55; NOAA National Marine Fisheries Service, pages 14, 15, 17 (top), 40, 43, 44, 47, 59; Museum of Modern Art, Film Stills Archive, pages 24, 27, 28, 32, 34, 37, 48, 52; San Diego Convention and Visitor's Bureau, page 56.


Published by Julian Messner, a Simon & Schuster
Division of Gulf & Western Corporation,
Simon & Schuster Building,
1230 Avenue of the Americas,
New York, New York 10020.


Manufactured in the United States of America.

Design by Regine de Toledo © 1982

Library of Congress Cataloging in Publication Data
Bunting, Eve, 1928–
The great white shark.

"A Jem book."
Bibliography: p.
Summary: Discusses theories about the origin
of the great white shark, its physical characteristics and behavior patterns, and ways to avoid a shark attack.
Includes index.
1. White shark—Juvenile Literature. [1. White
shark. 2. Sharks] I. Title.
QL638.95.L3B86 597'.31 82-3415
ISBN 0-671-44004-7 AACR2

# CONTENTS

# 1

# Rough Tooth, Huge Tooth

There was once a sea monster. It was about one hundred feet long. That's longer than a tennis court. Each tooth was as large as a man's hand. The monster could have swallowed a small Volkswagen car in one gulp.

Of course, there were no Volkswagens in those days. The creature's name was *Carcharodon Megalodon.* It lived in the ocean about 15 million years ago. Its name means rough tooth/huge tooth. And it is closely related to Carcharodon Carcharias—the great white shark.

Carcharodon Megalodon was the fiercest predator that ever lived. It was probably bigger and heavier than Tyrannosaurus rex, king of the giant lizards.

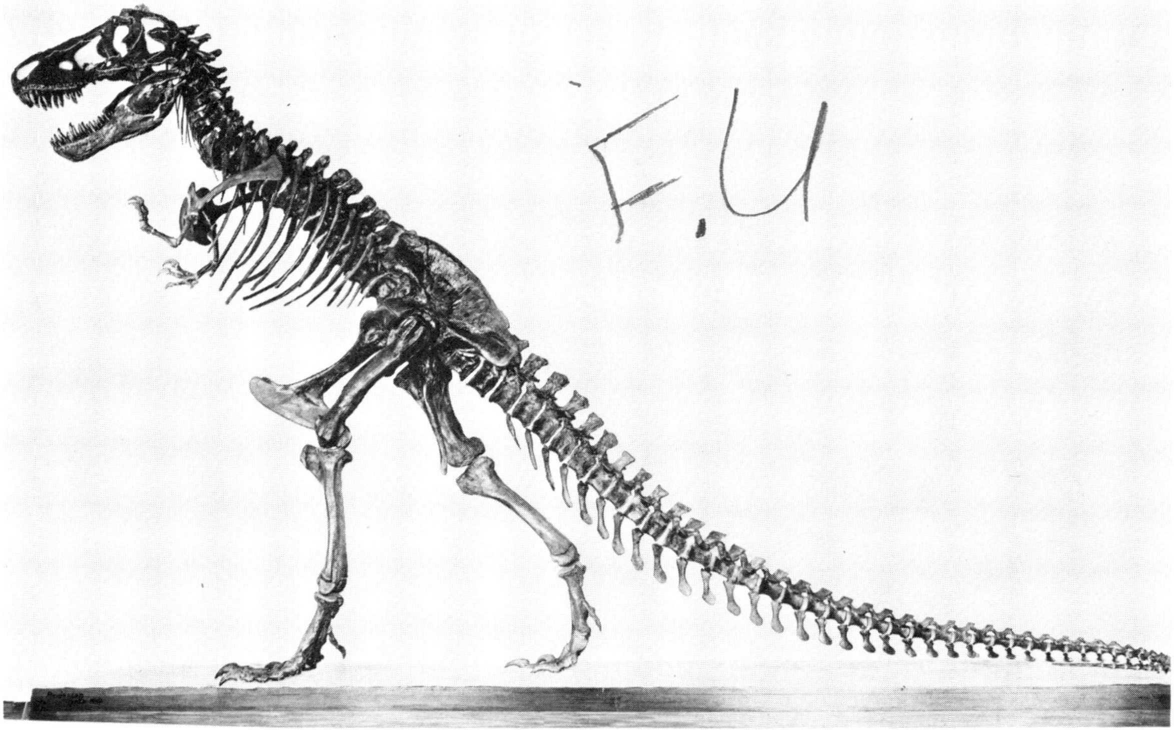

A skeleton of Tyrannosaurus rex

Like that giant dinosaur, Carcharodon Megalodon is now extinct, or is it? Some gigantic shark teeth were found in the Pacific Ocean not long ago. They were new teeth recently dropped from some giant jaw. They were too large to be from the great white shark. But they *were* shark teeth. Huge teeth as sharp as razors! What creature had lost them?

Fishermen often report seeing great white sharks bigger than any great white should be. Whales have been found covered with enormous shark bites. Were the bites made by great whites?

In 1918, fishermen at Port Stephens, Australia, saw a strange sight. It was "an immense shark." The creature came up and lifted their lobster pots. It swallowed the pots and the mooring lines, too. And those were big, heavy pots. Each one held close to forty large lobsters. The shark was like something from a nightmare. One man said it was 300 feet long. Another said it was as long as the dock they stood on. Its head was as "large as the roof" of the dock shed.

These fishermen knew the sea and its creatures. They knew what they'd seen. It was a "ghostly whitish" color, they said. It was a giant great white shark. Or perhaps it was the ancestor of the great white, Carcharodon Megalodon. There is no way to say for sure that the monster shark is still around. But there is no way to say for sure that it is not.

The sea keeps guard over its secrets. Who knows what lives in its mysterious depths?

In 1880, a Japanese fisherman pulled in an odd-looking shark. It was three and a half feet long. Its mouth was a beak. It had a broad, flat snout. No one had ever seen such a shark. People thought it was a new species. It was named after the man who found it. Then the scientists identified it. It was one of the species *Scapanorhynchus*. And that species had disappeared from earth about 100 million years ago. At least, it was supposed to have disappeared. If it still lives, Carcharodon Megalodon may still live, too.

There is a model in the American Museum of Natural History in New York. It shows the jaws of Carcharodon Megalodon. They are fearsome and terrifying. The teeth are set in rows like knives. There is a photograph of six men standing inside the jaws. There's room for a few more, too.

The preserved jaws of Carcharodon Carcharias—the great white—hang in the Natural History Museum in London. They are not as awesome as the jaws of Carcharodon Megalodon—smaller jaws, smaller teeth. But not small by any means. The teeth are two inches long. The jaws gape.

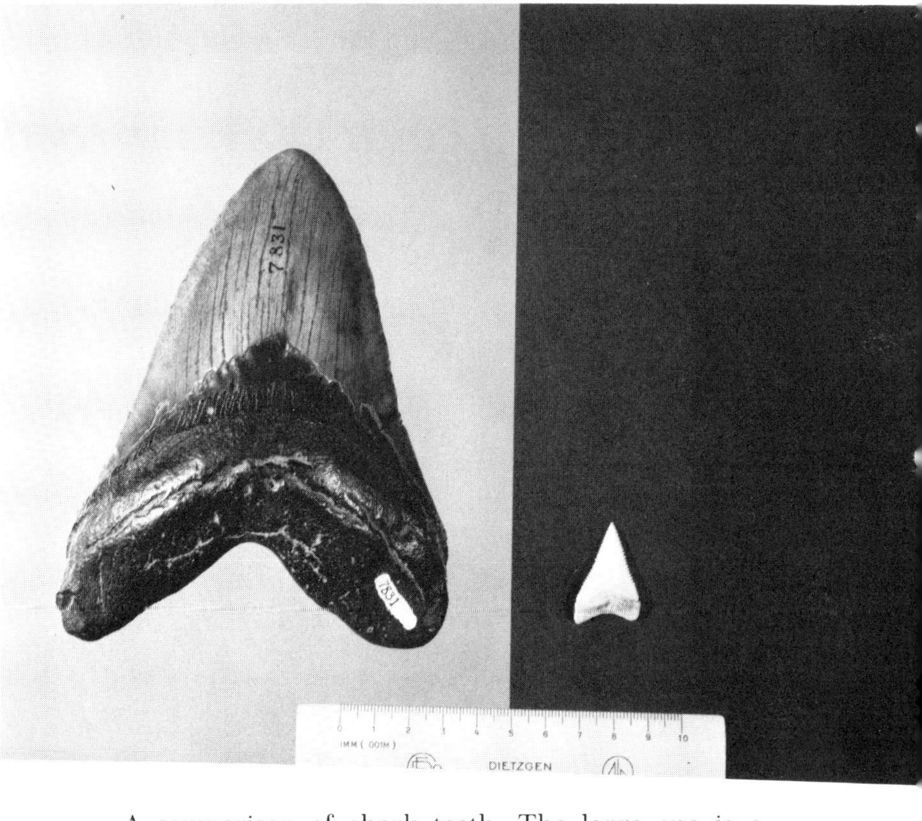


A comparison of shark teeth. The large one is a fossil. The small one was found off Florida.

A model of the jaws of Carcharodon Megalodon

It's easy to see what the French naturalist Rondolet meant. He wrote of a dead great white that he had seen. It had "a throat so big that a large and fat man could easily enter it," he wrote. Its throat was "such that if one held the mouth open, dogs could easily go inside to eat what they might find in the stomach."

Indeed! The largest great white ever caught was twenty-one feet long. It was found off Cuba. In 1976, a great white that was eighteen and a half feet long was caught off the coast of California. It was ten feet, two inches around the middle. Its jaws were big enough to have swallowed a human in one bite—probably even Rondolet's large and fat man!

In Australia, the great white is called the white pointer. In some parts of the world, it is called the great white death. It is known everywhere by its common name—the man-eater.

Great whites tend to act like lone wolves. They move about their business singly, not in schools. It is as though nature understands that one great white at a time is terror enough.

A man-eating white shark that was harpooned off Moriches Inlet, NY

DO IT ON THE
DO IT ON THE

# 2
# Big Whitey

All sharks are fish. Their skeletons are made of cartilage, not bone. Cartilage is rubbery and elastic.

Most fish have swim bladders. These keep them afloat. Sharks do not have swim bladders. They are heavier than water. Many of them must keep moving or they will sink.

It is the shark's liver that helps it stay afloat. The liver is huge and full of oil. Since oil is lighter than water, the liver floats. And the shark floats, too.

Sharks breathe by taking oxygen from the water and passing it through their gills. Their tails propel them through the water. The tail is

The mounted skin of a great white shark

A display model of assorted sharks

A whale shark

sometimes called the caudal fin. There are also dorsal, or back fins.

Sharks usually are dull colored. They look sleek and smooth. But they aren't. Shark skin is rough, covered with small sharp darts. These are called *denticles,* or skin teeth. It's true that a shark is "all teeth, from stem to stern." Don't rub against a shark! It's a good way to have your skin scraped from your body.

The teeth in the shark's jaw are its best weapons. They are sharp and dangerous. Strangely, they are set loosely in the gums. Often, when the shark bites, it leaves some teeth behind. But the shark doesn't have to worry. Other rows of teeth lie behind the ones in use.

When the front ones are lost, the others move forward.

The shark has a strong sense of smell. And the thing it smells most clearly in the water is blood. Blood excites a shark. It means fresh food. Experts are not sure if sharks feel hunger. But they sure like to eat. All they need to do is follow their noses if blood is nearby.

There is nothing wrong with a shark's eyesight. But they hunt mainly in the dark of oceans. In the passing of time, their other senses became more important. Sharks can "feel" noises in the water. They can sense electrical changes. All living things give off electricity. The shark can zero in on that, too.

A model of a whale shark

Sharks eat meat. That usually means fish, whales, seals, or other sharks. Sharks are cannibals. Some prefer shark meat to any other kind. One great white was harpooned off Monterey, California. A twenty-seven-pound piece of basking shark was stuck in its throat. Check out a twenty-seven-pound turkey some time. That's a hunk of meat! Another great white had two fully grown sharks in its stomach. One was six feet long, the other was seven feet. Great whites have attacked and killed humans. The shark may think the human is a juicy seal or sea lion. By then, it is too late for the human. And the killing makes the newspaper headlines.

The largest great white ever caught was twenty-one feet long. The smallest great white ever caught was fifty-one inches long. Its body is in a freezer in a laboratory in Rhode Island.

No female great white has been seen giving birth. Only one pregnant shark was ever found. When it was cut open, there were nine babies inside. Each one was two feet long.

Baby sharks are called pups. But these pups are not cuddly or playful. As soon as they are born, the pups are deadly sharks. They have full sets of teeth and will use them. They already have hunting instincts. The jaws of baby great whites are big. At a few months old, their mouths in relation to their body sizes are bigger than those of most adult sharks. Nature takes good care of shark pups. The mothers do not eat for a few days after birth. If they did, they would eat their own young. And after a while there would be no more sharks. The babies don't stick around and wait to be eaten. They get up and go!

Great whites are not the largest of the sharks. The basking shark and the whale shark are bigger. But the whale and the basking sharks are gentle creatures. They eat only plankton and small fish.

The great white will eat just about anything—kegs of nails or buoys. Whatever comes its way, it will eat. In sixteenth-century France, great whites were found that had "whole men in armor" in their stomachs. Had the soldiers been on a boat that sank? For sure, they weren't swimming—not in whole suits of armor.

The great white is a massive creature. It is shaped like a barrel. Still, it can move fast when it wants to. It is gray-brown above with a white belly. Its eyes are dark and deep. The rows of teeth are jagged and deadly. They are so sharp that Indians once used them for arrowheads.

Most people see the great white only in pictures. Other sharks can be kept in oceanariums, but not Big Whitey. It is too huge, too much a creature of the open sea. When put behind glass walls it dies. Perhaps that is another law of nature. Wild, fierce giants are not meant to be caged.

# 3

# The Mad Shark of New Jersey

*Jaws* is a book written by Peter Benchley. In 1974, it was made into a movie. Suddenly, half the world was swept by "Jaws" fever. Terror lurked in the oceans. Terror was a great white shark. It came close to shore and ate humans. The movie music was like a heart beating. It got louder as the shark swam closer to its victim. For weeks, people were afraid to swim in the ocean. The brave ones scoffed. "It couldn't happen. It's just a movie. Sharks don't do that kind of thing," they said.

Unfortunately, the brave ones were wrong. A few sharks have done that kind of thing. Something very like it did happen.

In July 1916, a great white shark killed four

A photograph from the movie, "Jaws"

people and attacked a fifth. The strikes were along the New Jersey coast. They lasted for ten days.

The first attack was on a twenty-four-year-old man. His name was Vansant. Vansant had been swimming in about five feet of water, close to shore. Other swimmers saw him standing in the surf. Then he began to scream. The water around him turned red. Several people went to help him. The first to reach him saw the shark—its jaws were still clamped on its victim. The rescuer began pulling Vansant to shore. Other swimmers came to help. Slowly, they dragged Vansant toward the beach. But the shark was coming, too! It wouldn't give up its grip on the victim's leg. When the people were in only one foot of water, the shark let go and swam away.

Vansant was lifted onto the sand. Unfortunately, the brave rescue was in vain. Vansant died a few hours after reaching the hospital.

Four days later, people on a nearby beach heard another man scream. He was quite far from shore. Two lifeguards set out in a boat to help him. They probably thought that he was having trouble in the surf. But he yelled to them that he'd been bitten by a shark.

The lifeguards carried him to the beach where he died within minutes. This second attack took place thirty-five miles from the first attack. It caused a panic. Shark watches were set up all along the coast. Beaches were netted to keep out what the papers called "the mad shark." Something had to be done.

Six days later, a man saw a big shark swimming in Matawan Creek. The creek was thirty miles from the place of the second shark attack. But it was away from the ocean. The man warned everyone who would listen. But no one believed him. After all, the creek was twenty miles in from the open sea. Besides, it was summer. It was hot. It was too hot to stay out of the water. And who ever heard of a shark in a creek?

When a ten-year-old boy began splashing and yelling, a man, Stanley Fisher, went to help him. The boy was an epileptic. It was easy to see that he needed help. Someone shouted a warning that it might be the shark. But Fisher went in anyway.

The boy had disappeared. Fisher dived and dived. At last he found the small figure. Cradling him in his arms, he started for shore. At first he swam. When it became shallow he waded, carrying the boy. Those on the beach saw him throw up his arms. He dropped the boy and began struggling. The people on the banks were screaming, "Shark! Shark!" But it was too late. Both the boy and Fisher had disappeared.

Men jumped into motorboats. But where should they look?

Then they saw Fisher again. He was drag-

A photograph from the movie, "Jaws." The shark is a mechanical model.

A white shark caught off Long Island

ging himself up on the bank. His wounds were terrible. He died later in the hospital.

The townspeople were frantic. There was a man-eater out there. It was decided to put dynamite in the water. But before they could begin their search for the shark, there was another tragedy.

A group of boys had been swimming in the creek. When they heard the awful word "Shark!" they rushed from the water. The last one out was twelve-year-old John Dunn. As he pulled himself up on the pier, the shark bit his left leg. It later had to be amputated. But John was lucky. He lost his leg and not his life. The ten-year-old epileptic boy lost his life. His body was found two days later. The shark had carried it upstream.

Now the hunt for the mad shark really began. Boatloads of men searched the creek. They fired bullets into any dark area. They dragged nets through the creek. And they caught smaller sharks. But none was a great white.

Then a great white was caught off South Amboy, New Jersey. In its stomach were human flesh and bones. One of the leg bones came from the second victim. There were no more attacks. It seemed that the killer had been killed.

Some shark experts believe that there are "rogue sharks." They do not behave like others of their kind. They are mad and behave like a rabid dog. That theory seems to fit here. Great whites do not usually go after humans. They prefer seals or whales. This one was different.

The story of "Jaws" was set in Amity, a sleepy little coastal town. There the rogue white shark terrorized the beaches.

"It couldn't happen," the brave ones said. They should read about the mad shark of New Jersey. The two stories were not that different. Except that the shark in "Jaws" was twenty-six feet long. The New Jersey great white was eight and a half feet long. For a killer, that is big enough.

# 4

# The Ones That Got Away

Not too many people meet a great white shark underwater. Some do, and they live to talk about it.

Jacques Cousteau is a famous oceanographer. He was diving one day when he came face to face with a great white. Cousteau thought his life was about to end. But the great white turned in the water and was gone. Who knows why? Perhaps Cousteau was simply lucky.

Brian Rodgers was not so lucky. In 1961, he was spearfishing with a friend, Rodney Fox. They were in the water off Adelaide, Australia. A white shark grabbed Brian from below. It took the lower part of his body in its mouth. Brian stabbed at the shark's eyes. He speared at the top

A photograph from the movie, "20,000 Leagues Under the Sea." The diver is a stuntman, but the shark is real.

of its head. The shark let go. But Brian's leg was ripped to shreds. He knew he would quickly bleed to death. Death from loss of blood is common after a shark bite. Brian wrapped the rubber sling of his spear gun around his leg. He began swimming for shore. He probably prayed that the shark was not swimming behind him. He probably expected to feel those teeth again. A rowboat picked him up. Brian's wounds needed three hours of surgery. But he did live.

Rodney Fox, who was with him, did not see the attack. He saw the great white, though. After it bit Brian, it swam toward Rodney. Then it turned and swam away. Who knows why? There are few answers to the mysteries of the great whites.

Rodney's luck held that day, but it didn't two years later. In 1963, he was spearfishing. There was a sudden quiet in the deep water around him. "It was a silence," he said. "Then something huge hit me on the left side. . . . I knew at once what had happened . . . and was dazed with horror." It was a great white.

Rodney reached behind him, trying to stab the shark's eyes. His arm went down the shark's throat. He pulled it out and felt the teeth rip strips off his skin. The shark let go and Rodney shot to the surface. Then he saw the shark beside him again with its jaws open. Rodney wrapped his arms and legs around the huge

A photograph from the movie, "The Sharkfighters." The sharks are only models.

body. The shark dived. Rodney held on with all his strength. He went under, too. The great white scraped its body on rocks. It felt the rider and wanted to be rid of him. Rodney let go and shot again to the surface. He had to have air. That is one of the terrors of a shark attack. The shark can breathe underwater.

The shark came back. Rodney had a fish float hooked to his belt. This time the shark grabbed the float. Rodney tried desperately to unhook his belt. But he couldn't. The shark's sharp teeth unhooked it for him. They cut clear through it. Rodney was free again. For the third time, he came to the surface. This time he saw a boat.

"Shark! Shark!" he yelled.

The men on the boat pulled him aboard.

It took 462 stitches and four hours of surgery to sew Rodney up. But he, too, lived.

Henri Bource was attacked while taking underwater pictures. It was November 1964, summertime in Australia. Henri and two friends were photographing seals. There were lots of seals around. But all at once they seemed to disappear.

"The water was quite empty," Henri said. "There was a split second of eerie silence."

The divers knew that something was wrong. They eased back toward the boat. But it was too late. It is probably always too late when that silence comes. Nature and its creatures helplessly wait.

The shark lifted Henri in its jaws right out of the water. He was able to scream "Shark!" before he was pulled under. The great white was shaking him. It was, Henri said, "the way a dog would shake an old slipper." Then it let him go.

When Henri got to the surface, he was missing his left leg. He was taken by boat to shore. An ambulance speeded him to the hospital. Henri also lived.

There is a second chapter to the Henri Bource story. And it is stranger than fiction. Henri got an artificial left leg. After some time, he was able to go back in the water. He began diving again. And in 1968, his left leg was bitten off for the second time by a great white shark. There was no blood this time. The shark ripped off Henri's artificial leg!

In 1976, Rob Rebstock was a student. He, his brother, and two friends were scuba diving off Santa Barbara, California. Rob jumped out of their boat. He trod water while his brother handed him his scuba gear. A great white shark shot up beneath Rob. It caught both his legs in its jaws and bit them together. Then it lifted itself and Rob out of the water and spat. Rob flew from its mouth and fell on his back. His brother and friends pulled him into the boat.

Rob had a three-by-five-inch hole in his

From the movie, "Jaws"

right thigh. There were six teeth marks in his left leg. The teeth had gone through the wet suit "clear to the bone." The shark did not chomp down on Rob. If it had, his legs would have been bitten off. It was a horror for Rob. It was a horror, too, for those in the boat.

They were five lucky people. They were five of the rare breed, "the ones that got away!"

The human spirit is strong. Jacques Cousteau still makes underwater dives. He shares with us the secrets of the oceans. Brian Rodgers enjoys deep-sea shark fishing. Rodney Fox still dives. He leads groups on the search for the great white shark. Henri Bource is a professional diver. He works on off-shore oil rigs and has made shark films. Sometimes he leaves his artificial leg on shore when he dives! Today, Rob Rebstock is an attorney. He lives in Santa Barbara so he can be "near the water." He still surfs and dives in the same ocean where Big Whitey grabbed him in 1976.

These are ocean people, lovers of the sea. They will not allow themselves to be scared away. Perhaps they feel there is little danger of another attack. Lightning is not supposed to strike twice in the same place. But it struck Henri Bource twice. The lightning was a great white shark, rising from the dark depths.

# 5

# They Search for Sharks

Most people don't go looking for sharks. And they hope sharks don't come looking for them. But there are some men and women who do search for sharks. They may want to "tag" them. They may want to kill them, or photograph them, or simply admire them.

Tagging a shark means placing a tag in its dorsal fin. Then the shark is released. If it is caught again, the tag is found. The finder answers the questions on the tag. How big is the shark? Where was it found? When was it found? The tag and the answers are returned to the researchers. They can learn about shark growth from the new information. They can find out how far sharks travel and where. One tag was

Men weighing a small white shark

returned from a blue shark. The animal had gone 2,700 miles in four months!

Tagging was once a risky business for both man and shark. First, the shark had to be caught. Then it was lifted into a boat. The tag was hooked on its fin. The size of the great whites made tagging them impossible. It was difficult with any shark. Sharks are strong in the water. They fight desperately for life. There are stories of sharks, gutted and thrown back. Even then, they continued to swim.

There are stories of sharks that have had their jaws sliced out. When put back in the ocean, they still swam. But sharks are sensitive to handling. Their bodies are always supported by water. Their insides have little protection from the hard boards of boats. Even when carefully lifted, a tagged shark often dies.

Jack Casey, a marine biologist, developed the dart tag. A dart is fixed on a long pole. The tag is on the dart. The shark can be jabbed while it is still in the water. Tagging is suddenly easy. Now it is widely used. We can learn more about sharks. We may even come to understand the great whites.

Frank Mundus also searches the oceans for sharks. He especially hopes to find great whites. Mundus lives in Montauk, Long Island. He runs a charter boat for those who want to catch sharks. The prize take is always a great white.

Why would anyone want to catch a great white? Perhaps it is human nature to want to capture the man-eater. A fisherman feels powerful. He is catching the most powerful fish of all. There is, perhaps, revenge. This shark may have eaten people. It serves him right to be caught and killed. There is the thrill of catching him. This is dangerous sports fishing. And think how great that head will look, mounted on the wall!

Not too many fishermen would want to get in the water with Big Whitey. It's all right from a boat. That way all the risk is to the shark.

Certainly, many fishermen want to try for a shark. Mundus's boat, the *Cricket* 2, is booked a year ahead. Near the rail is a box with a dragon painted on it. On the box are the words, MONSTER MASH. The box holds the bait to catch the sharks. Shark bait is called *chum*. When it is dropped overboard, the search for sharks is on. The fishermen are then chumming for shark. Usually, the bait is a mixture of whale oil and hunks of goat, sheep, or horse. There may be minced tuna.

Mundus is good at finding sharks. He himself harpooned a massive great white. It was seventeen and a half feet long. Shot with five harpoons, it dragged the *Cricket* 2 for five hours. It seemed that it would never give up. Not yet dead, it was pulled up on the beach with a bulldozer. A rifle shot finished it off.

Measuring a 1,500-pound white shark caught off Montauk, NY

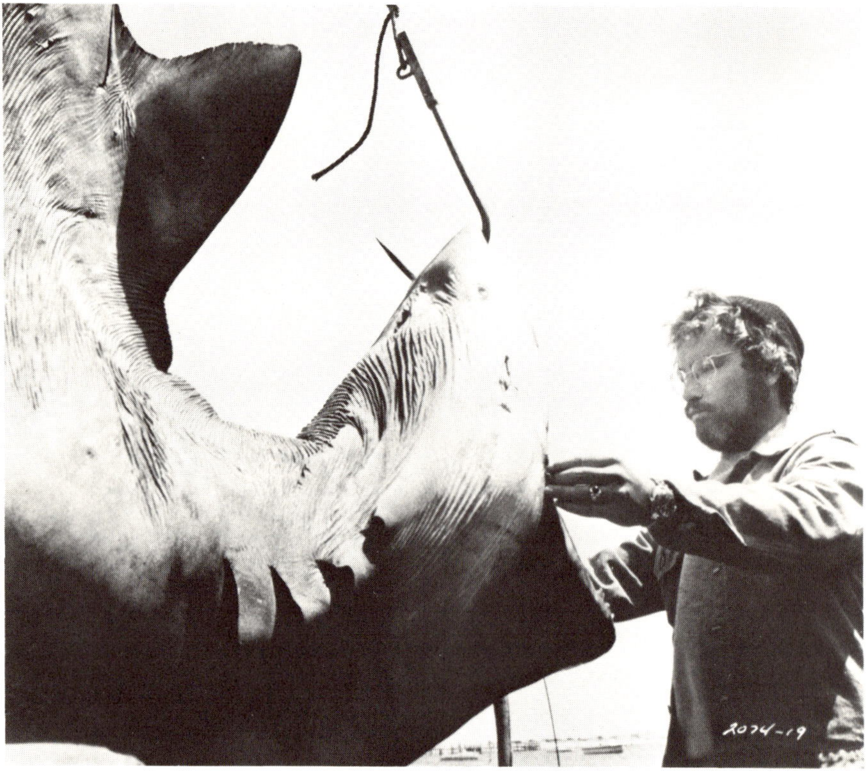


From the movie, "Jaws"

The head of Mundus's great white shark hangs in a bar in Montauk. It is the heaviest great white ever caught. The giant fish probably weighed 4,200 pounds. The word "probably" has to be used. There are few scales big enough to hold a great white.

One of Mundus's customers was Peter Benchley, who wrote *Jaws.* Many people think that Quint, the shark fisherman in the book, is like Mundus.

Frank Mundus says that he does not hate sharks. He does not love them, either. He has fun fishing for them, that's all. He also says that it is harder now to find great whites. They are rare and getting rarer. It seems a shame to keep killing them off just for fun. It's a waste to kill them just for a set of jaws to show off to friends. Some shark meat is good to eat. But there's one safe bet. Mundus's fishermen are not simply looking for shark steaks.

Ron and Val Taylor are husband and wife. They hunt for sharks to photograph them. The Taylors are among the best underwater photographers in the world. Check any picture of a great white in action. The chances are it was taken by a Taylor.

In 1974, *Jaws* was turned into a movie. A lifelike shark was made in the studio. This would be used for some of the shots. But the filmmakers wanted pictures of a real great white, too. It would make the movie seem less fake. True shots would be mixed with those of the manmade shark.

"Jaws" was to be an American movie. The Taylors are Australian. But they are the best. So they were asked to do the underwater work.

From the beginning, Ron and Val knew it wouldn't be easy. Their friend, Peter Gimbel, is also a wonderful photographer. He had filmed great whites for his movie, "Blue Water, White Death." The Taylors had worked with him. Underwater shark cages were used. These were strong, steel cages that were hung over the side of a boat. The photographers worked inside the cages. While they rolled the cameras, the great whites chomped on the chum around them. They chomped on the cages, too, and on the keel of the boat. They bit so hard that their teeth broke off. At the time, Peter Gimbel said: "Those animals were trying to eat us, no question about it."

The Taylors would use cages to film the sharks for "Jaws." But there was one extra problem. The director didn't want cage bars in some of the shots. He wanted Big Whitey snapping right at the camera! It was decided that Ron would work outside the cage. He would stand by the cage door. If the great white looked dangerous, Ron would swim inside.

It's hard to know when a great white

A female white shark caught off Amagansett, NY.
Those teeth are very sharp!

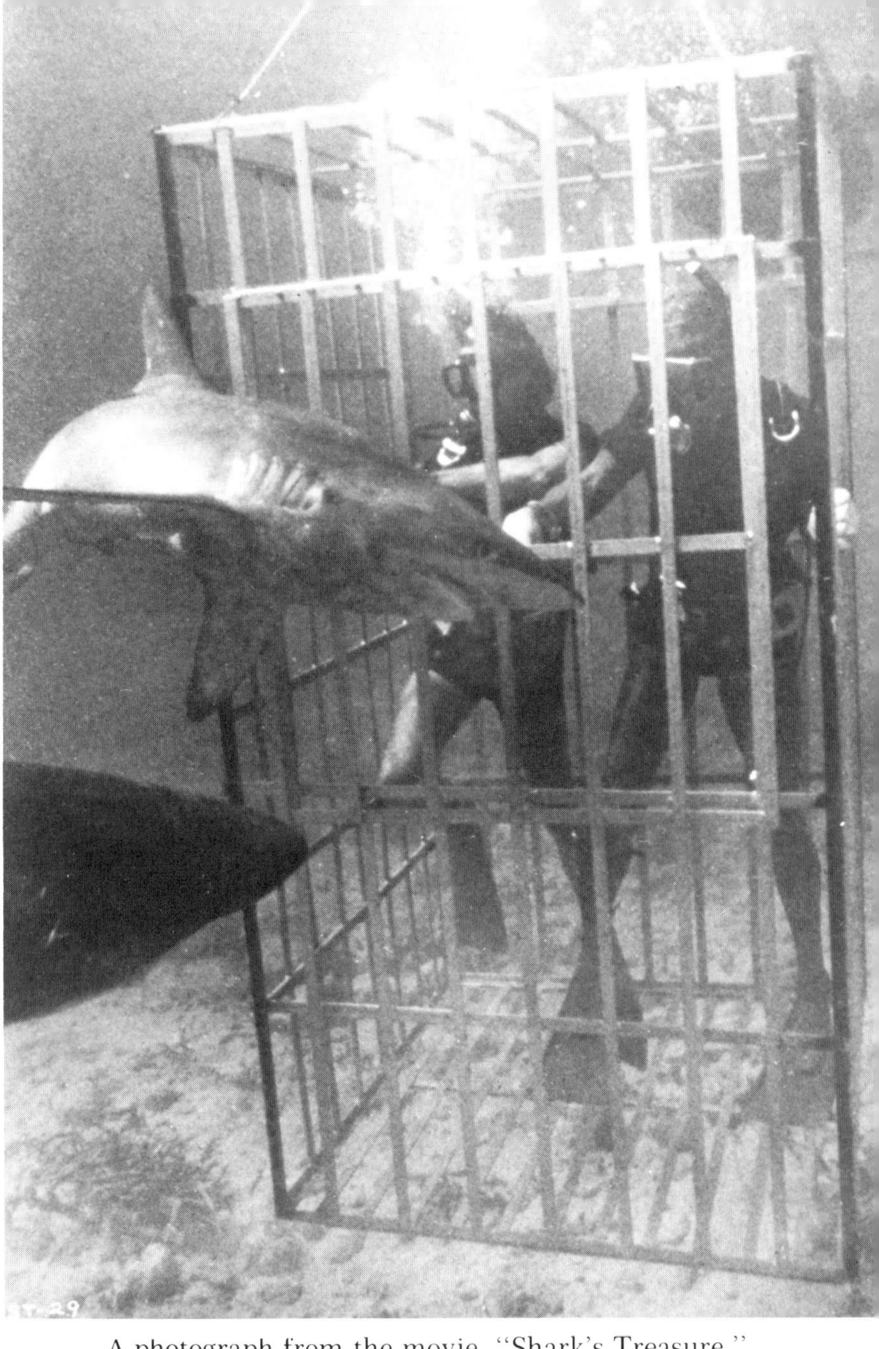

A photograph from the movie, "Shark's Treasure." The divers are protected by a shark cage.

wouldn't look dangerous. But Ron has photographed hundreds of sharks—maybe thousands. He can read shark signs. He has hung over the edge of a boat to take pictures of the man-eater. His arms and head have been underwater, close to those fearful jaws. Once, while filming, he fell overboard. Below him were three great whites feeding on half a horse. The dead horse had been placed there for bait. Ron managed to get safely back aboard. He is a lucky man. He would need his luck for this new adventure.

The Taylors set off with their crew and their friend Rodney Fox. They anchored off Dangerous Reef to wait. The reef is fourteen miles off the southern Australian coast. If the Great White Death is to be found, it will be found there.

On the second day, the first great white came. Ron climbed on to the backboard of the boat. The shark moved in to feed. In the movie, the great white has scars on its nose. Rodney Fox leaned down. Using Val's lipstick, he painted "scars" where they should be. And Rodney Fox had once needed 462 stitches for a shark bite! Like Ron, Rodney has courage.

Some filming was done from the cages. Some was done outside of them. Ron was once sitting on top of the cage with the camera rolling. Three great whites came from the depths. Val could see them from above. She was frantic.

From the movie, "Shark's Treasure"

Three great whites at once were too many. Why didn't Ron get back in the cage? One great white swam silently toward him. Ron hit it on the snout with his camera. The giant shark swam away. Ron explained later. He couldn't get back in the cage. His diving harness had tangled in the wire! Ron's luck held that day, too.

The success of "Jaws" owes much to the Taylor's cameras. The sharks look real because many of them are.

Val and Ron also lead tourist expeditions to search for Big Whitey. There are people who want to go down in shark cages. They want to see the Great White Death swimming freely. They are willing to pay a lot of money to do it.

Four men went on the first tour in 1976. Afterwards, Valerie asked one of them if it had been worth the money. He said yes.

"I'll never forget it. Those sharks are the most beautiful things I've seen."

These men were free of fear and protected by steel. They could marvel at the great whites' grace and power. They could see the giant shark for what it is—one of the living wonders of the world.

A display model of a coral reef

# 6

# Shark Protection

If you meet a shark in the water, what should you do? Experts disagree. Some say stay quiet. Make no noise to excite the shark. Try not to show fear. Sharks can sense fear in the way that a dog can. Other experts say to splash. That may scare the shark away. If possible, rap it on the nose with something heavy—a camera, if you have one with you, a spear, a diving mask. Only use your fist if you have nothing else. The shark's sandpaper skin may scrape your hand. And you don't want blood in the water. Poke at its eyes. Look aggressive. There's an old saying: "Doctors differ and patients die." With sharks, it is: "Experts differ and swimmers could die."

There are some things you should not do:

1) Don't swim at night. That is when most shark attacks occur.
2) Don't swim in murky water. Sharks like to prowl where the water is muddy.
3) Don't dive or swim close to rocks where seals live. Seals and sea lions are a shark's food. Great whites patrol those areas. A shark can mistake a swimmer for a seal. Even if it spits you out, it may be too late. Everyone is not as lucky as Rob Rebstock.
4) Don't go in the ocean if you have a bleeding wound. Experts say a scratch will not attract a shark. Flowing blood will bring them.
5) If you are spearfishing, don't trail the speared fish in the water. Take them out immediately. Under no circumstances tie the dead fish to your waist. If a shark comes to feed, he won't know which is the fish and which is you.

Valerie Taylor, in her book *Great Shark Stories,* gives some advice to surfers.

"If I were a surfboard rider, I would paint

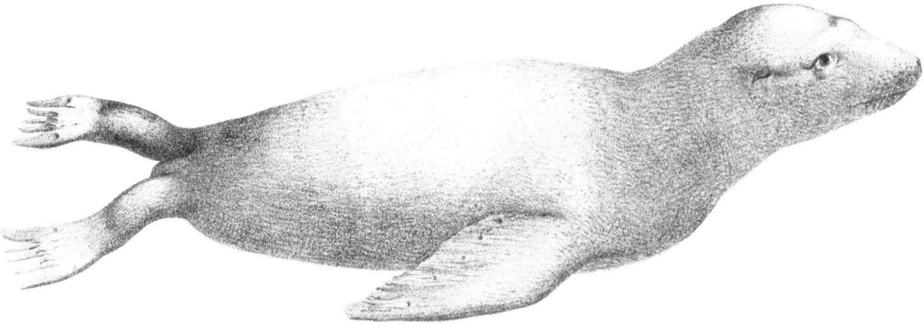

Sharks like to eat seals.

Surfers have to beware of sharks.

two mean-looking eyes on the bottom of my board. Sharks don't like being looked at." She also repeats what she told her nephews. They seem to be ocean lovers, too. If they meet up with a shark, they should put their heads under the water and look at it. They may not be able to see a thing. But the shark won't know that. "Having your dinner look you in the eye can be . . . worrisome," Val says. She advises them to "punch and kick, especially at the eyes and gills. Everything should be tried. Fight, don't just give in."

Rules that apply to average sharks don't always apply to the great white. It is so big and merciless. Peter Gimbel, the shark photographer, says, "The great white is different. Other sharks bump and nudge first. The white's first move is to bite. It doesn't circle, but comes straight at you." Still, Ron Taylor drove one away with a whack on the snout.

Some shores seem very attractive to sharks. Many ways have been tried to protect these dangerous beaches. One method was the "bubble curtain." The bubble curtain was a long hose with holes in it. The hose was stretched under the water some distance from shore. When air was pumped through, it made rising bubbles. This bubble wall was between the beach and the open sea. The shark was not supposed to cross it.

The bubble curtain was made and tested in a laboratory. Twelve tiger sharks were used in the experiment. One was stopped by the bubbles. The others swam through them, time and time again. One gave up, eleven didn't. These are not very good odds! It seems that sharks, like people, aren't all afraid of the same things.

The beaches off South Africa used to be prime targets for sharks. Then the beaches were netted. Many nets were set in overlapping rows beyond the beach in the water. Each net was twenty feet high. It was weighted and reached to the bottom. It cut off the shore from the open sea. The sharks got trapped in the nets. When they can't swim, they can't breathe. They quickly drown.

In the years from 1966 to 1972, more than 7,000 sharks were caught in South African nets. Of those, 143 were great whites. There have been only six attacks on the protected beaches.

But there is one strange fact. Many sharks have been caught going out of the netted area. Somehow they got through. They swam with the swimmers and left. This seems to prove what Richard Ellis says. If sharks wanted to eat people, "the world's oceans would be dyed crimson with the blood of millions."

All beaches cannot be netted. Divers dive in the open sea. Surfers surf. Swimmers swim. Airplanes crash in the oceans. Ships sink. Boats turn over. The search goes on for good protection.

A male white shark caught off Moriches Inlet, NY

The "shark screen" may help. It is a large, heavy, plastic bag. It could be used after ship or plane disasters. The person floats inside the bag. The shark can't see or smell what's inside. He should swim on by. But what if he's nosey and takes a bite?

One chemical called "shark chaser" was used for a time by the navy and air force. Poison was shot into the water. But the shark chaser did not work too well. Spears, powerheads, and darts are used by divers. Some carry a "shark billy." This is a wooden stick with a nail on the end. It can be used to fend off sharks. There are underwater guns that will kill a shark instantly. But most ordinary swimmers and divers don't take a gun with them in the water.

A striped wet suit was invented for divers. It looked like the skin of a poisonous sea snake. Sharks would stay away from it, the inventor said. Some sharks did, but some didn't. It was the old story. Sharks never do what they are expected to do.

Dr. Eugenie Clark has studied sharks for years. One of her finds may be of great importance. There is a small fish that is found in the Red Sea. Its name is the Moses sole. In its fins is a milky liquid. This liquid seems to "freeze" open a shark's jaws. When the shark tries to bite a Moses sole its mouth won't close. What is this strange liquid? Can it be taken from the Moses sole? Can it be used by humans against sharks?

Meantime, fact and fiction go hand in hand. It is said that the color orange attracts sharks. Never wear orange in shark-infested waters. That includes a life jacket. Never wear yellow. Sharks love that color. In shark circles, it's called "yum-yum yellow"! Great whites have been seen swimming past floating food. They headed straight for a yellow buoy and attacked it over and over again.

Paul Budker, a French shark expert, says that fleas, lice, and mosquitos carry diseases. Therefore they are "more to be feared than sharks." But you can spray a mosquito and kill it dead. There's no shark spray yet. And most of us would prefer a flea bite to a shark bite. The great white shark is the most terrifying creature in today's world—and one of the most wonderful.

# Index

# Bibliography

Budker, Paul. *The Life of Sharks.* New York: Columbia University Press, 1971.

Bunting, Eve. *The Sea World Book of Sharks.* See World Press, 1979.

Cousteau, Jacques-Yves, and Cousteau, Phillipe. *The Shark: Splendid Savage of the Sea.* Garden City, NY: Doubleday and Co., 1970.

Ellis, Richard. *The Book of Sharks.* New York: Grosset and Dunlap, 1976.

Taylor, Ron, and Taylor, Valerie. *Great Shark Stories.* New York: Harper and Row, 1978.

# About the Author

Eve Bunting has written more than a hundred books for young people, both fact and fiction.

She has always been fascinated by the sea and has done books on its other mysterious creatures, the giant squid and the great whales.

Mrs. Bunting lives in California and has three grown-up children.